LANGUAGE-ARTS EXPLORER

THE TRANSFER OF ENERGY

by Christine Zuchora-Walske

SCIENCE LAB:
THE TRANSFER OF ENERGY

CHERRY LAKE PUBLISHING • ANN ARBOR, MICHIGAN

CHERRY LAKE Publishing

Published in the United States of America
by Cherry Lake Publishing
Ann Arbor, Michigan
www.cherrylakepublishing.com

Printed in the United States of America
Corporate Graphics Inc
September 2011
CLFA09

Consultants: Peter Barnes, assistant scientist, University of Florida; Gail Saunders-Smith, associate professor of literacy, Beeghly College of Education, Youngstown State University

Editorial direction: Book design and illustration:
Lisa Owings   Kazuko Collins

Photo credits: Rafa Irusta/Fotolia, cover, 1; Steven King/AP Images, 5; Shutterstock Images, 7; Igor Profe/Fotolia, 9; Stephen Sweet/Fotolia, 11; Diane Bondareff/AP Images, 14; Fotolia, 17, 24; Zacarias Pereira da Mata/Shutterstock Images, 18; Lynn Schommer/Bigstock, 21; Daniel Korzeniewski/Shutterstock Images, 27

Library of Congress Cataloging-in-Publication Data
Zuchora-Walske, Christine.
Science lab. The transfer of energy / by Christine Zuchora-Walske.
      p. cm. – (Language arts explorer. Science lab)
Includes index.
ISBN 978-1-61080-209-3 – ISBN 978-1-61080-298-7 (pbk.)
1. Energy transfer–Juvenile literature. I. Title. II. Title: Transfer of energy.
QC73.8.E53Z83 2011
531'.6–dc23
                        2011015134

Cherry Lake Publishing would like to acknowledge the work of The Partnership for 21st Century Skills. Please visit www.21stCenturySkills.org for more information.

TABLE OF CONTENTS

Your Mission 4

What You Know 4

What Is Energy? 6

Wind Turbines 10

Chemical Reactions 14

Photosynthesis 18

Energy Conservation 22

Mission Accomplished! 26

Consider This 26

Glossary 28

Learn More 29

Further Missions 30

Index 31

You are being given a mission. The facts in What You Know will help you accomplish it. Remember the clues from What You Know while you are reading the story. The clues and the story will help you answer the questions at the end of the book. Have fun on this adventure!

Energy exists in everything. It moves through the universe constantly, often changing form along the way. This movement is called **energy transfer**. Your mission is to investigate how energy transfer happens. What is energy, and how do scientists study it? What are its many forms, and how does it change from one form to another? What kinds of experiments help us understand what energy can do? Read the facts in What You Know and begin your mission to explore the process of energy transfer.

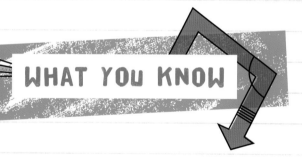

WHAT YOU KNOW

★ **Energy** exists in all matter. Matter is any physical substance.

★ Energy is the ability to change matter or do work. Work is done when a force moves an object.

★ Matter in motion has **kinetic energy**. **Potential energy** is the energy matter has because of its position or how its parts are arranged.

The static electricity produced by a Van de Graaff generator can make your hair stand on end. Electricity is just one form of energy.

★ Energy cannot be created or destroyed. It can only change form or location. This change is called energy transfer.

★ Every interaction between things transfers energy.

Anna Patel is attending Energy Camp at her local science museum. She and her fellow campers investigate what energy is, how it changes, and what it can do. Carry out your mission by reading her journal.

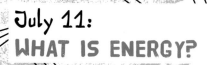
Today was my first day at camp. Our leader is Reynaldo—Rey for short. Rey said when he's not leading Energy Camp, he's an engineer for a wind power company. He helps design and build wind **turbines**—like those big windmills we see when we drive out in the country. First we introduced ourselves and toured the museum. Then we went outside.

Kinetic Energy

Rey asked us to sit quietly on the lawn and observe our surroundings. He said observing is studying carefully. "What moving things do you notice?" he asked.

Here are some of the things I noticed:

1. I saw Tony, the boy next to me, scratch his ear.
2. I felt the wind blowing my hair into my face.
3. I saw a lady jogging while pushing a baby in a stroller.
4. I felt a mosquito bite my ankle.

After a few minutes, Rey said, "Think about the motion you noticed. What did it accomplish?"

I was confused at first. I thought about Rey's question some more. Here's what I realized:

When you feel the wind in your hair, you are feeling kinetic energy at work.

1. Tony's scratching fingers wiggled his ear and made red marks on his skin.

2. The blowing wind moved my hair from the side of my face to the front.

3. The lady's jogging legs pushed her body, her stroller, and her baby forward.

4. The mosquito's biting mouth made a tiny hole in my skin.

I spoke up: "Each moving thing did some kind of work. It moved another thing, or it made some other kind of change."

"Aha!" said Rey. "Energy is the ability to change matter or do work. So if motion can move or change things, then motion is a kind of energy. It's called kinetic energy."

Potential Energy

"There are two main kinds of energy," Rey went on. "Kinetic energy is one. Potential energy is the other. Potential energy is the energy matter has because of its position or how its parts are arranged."

I had no idea what Rey meant by that. I was glad when he suggested some activities to help us understand potential energy. Here's what I tried:

★ I stretched a rubber band and aimed it at a nearby tree. Then I let go. The rubber band went flying.

ROLLER COASTERS

Roller coasters are powered by a combination of potential and kinetic energy. As a roller coaster climbs each hill, its potential energy builds. The potential energy turns into kinetic energy as gravity pulls the coaster down the steep drops. By switching from potential to kinetic energy and back again, roller coasters have enough energy to keep you screaming until the end of the ride.

When you pick up a rock, you are giving it gravitational energy. Gravitational energy is a form of potential energy.

Rey said rubber is elastic—it tries to keep its normal shape. Stretching the rubber band gave it elastic potential energy. Letting go released that energy.

★ I picked up a rock with my hand. Then I let go, and the rock fell to the ground. Rey explained that Earth's gravity pulled it down. Gravity is a force that causes every object to pull on every other object. Lifting the rock gave it gravitational potential energy. Letting go released that energy.

Today I learned that energy is all around me. But I wonder—what kinds of things can energy do? ★

Rey took us on a field trip today. We visited the company where he works. As we walked toward the building, I saw several spinning objects sticking out from the sides and up from the roof. Some looked like fans. Others looked like eggbeaters. The spinners were different shapes and sizes.

From Air to Electricity

Rey pointed to the spinners and said, "Those are wind turbines. They change the wind's energy into electricity. My coworkers and I use that electricity to run our computers, light our lights, and so on."

Rey took us inside, and we climbed the stairs to the roof. We gathered near a short, fan-shaped turbine. Its casing was clear plastic, so we could see both the outer and inner parts.

Rey explained, "This turbine has three main parts: a rotor, a shaft, and a generator. The rotor looks like a fan. It's a set of blades attached to a central piece called a hub. As wind pushes against the blades, they move. This movement makes the hub spin. The hub is attached to a rod called the shaft. As the hub spins, so does the shaft.

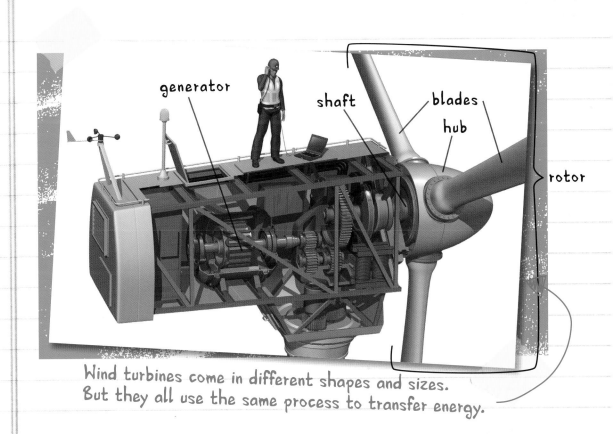

generator   shaft   blades   hub   rotor

Wind turbines come in different shapes and sizes.
But they all use the same process to transfer energy.

The spinning shaft is attached to an electric generator. The generator contains a set of strong magnets that spin inside many coils of metal wire. As the shaft spins the magnets inside the generator, the magnets push **electrons** through the wire. The flowing electrons create an electric current within the wire."

Rey said that energy transfer happens inside the turbine. That means the turbine changes the form or location of energy. "In fact," he said, "energy changes several times in a turbine. See if you can name the energy transfers."

ELECTRICITY

When electrons move among different atoms, they create a current of electricity. This is what happens inside a wind turbine's generator. The spinning magnets push electrons in the metal wire, making them jump from one atom to the next. The movement creates an electric current that flows from one end of the wire to the other. Since an electric current comes from the energy of electrons in motion, it is a form of kinetic energy.

Here's what my friends and I came up with:

1. The blowing wind moves the turbine blades.
2. The moving blades spin the hub.
3. The spinning hub makes the shaft spin.
4. The spinning shaft moves the magnets.
5. The magnets push electrons in the wire to make an electric current.

Capturing the Wind

Rey told us the turbines actually do two jobs. "They make electricity for our building, of course. But they also give us information. We study how much electricity the different turbines make in different conditions. Then we use what we know to design new wind turbines."

Rey explained that engineers can experiment with the different features in a turbine. For example, they can change the number of blades, the size of the blades, the way the blades face the wind, or the height of the turbine.

Rey and his coworkers—and other engineers around the world—have built turbines with many different designs. And they've tried out their designs in many different places, from flat prairies to mountaintops and from crowded cities to open seas. They've learned that different designs work better in some places than in others.

"For example," said Rey, "a giant turbine works great in a big open area with steady wind. It might have blades as long as school buses on top of a 300-foot (90 m) tower. It captures a lot of wind and makes a lot of electricity. But here in the city, space is tight. And the wind is unpredictable. It comes and goes and swirls around. Even if we had enough room for a giant turbine here, the wind wouldn't budge it. Cities need different kinds of turbines. My coworkers and I design turbines that fit in crowded spaces and spin even in light, swirling winds."

Today I learned that one type of kinetic energy can change into another type of kinetic energy. But I wonder—can potential energy change into kinetic energy? ★

July 15:
CHEMICAL REACTIONS

We started camp outside this morning. Rey set up supplies on the sidewalk.

From Fuel to Flight

Rey gave each of us a small plastic container with a snap-on lid. We each put one teaspoon of baking powder into our container. Then we poured in a little bit of water and snapped the lid on right away. We shook our containers, set them upside down on the ground, and backed up quickly. In

A chemical reaction between Mentos candy and diet soda causes the soda to shoot into the air!

a few seconds, the containers all popped away from their lids and shot into the air like rockets.

I jumped. So did the other kids. We turned to Rey, confused. How did a little powder and water become rocket fuel?

Rey explained, "Baking powder contains cream of tartar, which is an acid, and baking soda, which is a base. The two don't mix unless they get wet. When you poured water in the container, it mixed the acid and base. When an acid and base mix, a chemical reaction takes place. That means their **molecules** break up. Their atoms rearrange into new kinds of molecules. A chemical reaction between baking soda, cream of tartar, and water forms bubbles of carbon dioxide gas."

"But how did the containers fly in the air?" I asked.

Rey continued, "In any substance, the molecules move around. Gas molecules move around faster than liquid ones. Inside your closed container, the gas molecules were literally bouncing off the walls. As your mixture formed more and more gas, the bouncing gas molecules pushed harder and harder on the insides of the container. That pushing is called pressure. Finally the pressure popped off the lid and shot the container into the air like a rocket.

DIGESTION

When you eat a piece of cake, or any food, chemicals in your body's digestive system react with the chemicals in the food. This reaction releases chemical energy that your body uses to move and grow.

"Your rocket demonstrated energy transfer," said Rey. "Chemical energy is a type of potential energy. You turned the chemical energy of baking powder and water into the kinetic energy of a flying container."

Baking the Perfect Cake

We cleaned up our mess. Then we walked a few city blocks to the headquarters of Bakewell. That's a company that makes dry baking products, such as cake mixes.

We rode the elevator up to a huge open room called a test kitchen. It looked like a kitchen and a laboratory combined. The workers all wore matching lab coats. Some were gathering ingredients from fridges and cupboards. Others were measuring and mixing or baking and tasting. Everybody was taking notes.

Maria, the test kitchen director, explained that her employees are experts in both food science and cooking. Part

The chemical energy of baking powder gives cake its fluffy texture.

of their work is to find out what combinations of ingredients make baked goods with perfect flavors and textures.

For example, one person was working on a lemon cake mix. He was puzzling out the right amount of each ingredient—flour, sugar, lemon flavoring, baking powder, and so on—to make a cake that tastes lemony but not sour and that bubbles enough when mixed with water so it will bake into a fluffy cake. His job was tricky. Both lemon and baking powder contain acids. Too much of either, and the cake tasted sour. Too little of either, and the cake batter didn't bubble enough. It baked into a flat, heavy cake. After many tries, he found just the right combination.

Today I learned that potential energy can change into kinetic energy. But I wonder—are there other kinds of energy? ★

Today we explored the museum grounds. Rey led us around to the back lawn, where the museum hosts a community garden. People who live in the neighborhood share this garden. Most of them live in apartment buildings or condos, so they have no yards. If they want to, they can grow flowers, herbs, vegetables, and fruits here.

Sugar Factory

Along one side of the garden fence we saw tall, lush blackberry bushes. The branches were heavy with berries. Some were green, pink, or red. But many were dark purple.

Plants are the only living things that can use photosynthesis to turn energy from the sun into food.

Rey showed us four photos of the bushes taken earlier this year. One was labeled "March." It showed small brown twigs peeking out of the snow and mud. The next photo said "April." In this one, the snow was gone. The bushes were still small, but they had buds and some little leaves. In the photo labeled "May," the bushes were taller and leafier. The last photo read "June." In this one, the bushes were big and bushy and very green. We could see some green berries too.

Rey explained how the little brown twigs in the first photo became the big green berry-filled bushes in front of us. He said, "A blackberry plant, like all plants, gets the

PLANT POWER

The molecules that make up a plant contain chemical energy. Eventually that energy changes location or form. For example, an animal might eat the plant. Digestion releases the plant's chemical energy to help the animal grow and function. Or a plant might become fuel. For example, a person might burn wood for light and heat. Humans can also process plants to make fuel for machines.

Coal, oil, and natural gas are fuels processed by nature. These fuels formed from ancient plant and animal material buried underground. Over millions of years, heat and pressure changed the material into fuels crammed with chemical energy.

energy it needs through a process called photosynthesis. Photosynthesis is a kind of energy transfer. It changes energy from the sun into the chemical energy of food. A plant is basically a sugar factory."

He continued, "Here's how it works: A plant absorbs sunlight. Sunlight is a form of electromagnetic energy, which is different from kinetic or potential energy. The plant also takes in water and carbon dioxide from the air and soil. The energy from sunlight triggers a chemical reaction in the plant. The water and carbon dioxide molecules break up and rearrange into sugar and oxygen molecules. The plant releases the oxygen into the air. It uses the sugar as food so it can grow and function."

I could see that the blackberry bushes had been busy sugar factories this summer. They were taller than me, and they had tons of berries! "Do the bushes always grow that big?" I asked.

Just Right

"Nope," Rey answered. "The museum staff planted these bushes about six years ago. They grow back on their own every year. One year we had too much rain and not enough sunshine. Another year was too hot and dry. In those years the bushes were wimpy, and they didn't

Very dry soil is just right for gaillardias. Other plants need different conditions to make food and grow.

produce many berries. Other plants in the garden did well though. See those yellow irises?" He pointed to some tall yellow flowers. "They love soggy soil. They grew like crazy during that rainy year. Those gaillardias over there," he said, pointing to some bright red-and-yellow daisies, "grew better when it was hot and dry."

I realized that a plant needs just the right amounts of water and sunshine to make plenty of food for itself. I could also see that different kinds of plants needed different conditions to grow. ★

It was stormy today, so we stayed inside. We explored energy conservation in the museum lab.

From Coal to Electricity

Rey explained, "Most of this building's electricity comes from coal. Changing coal into electricity takes several steps. Energy transfer happens during each step."

1. At a power plant, a furnace burns the coal.
2. The burning coal's heat boils water.
3. The boiling water produces steam.
4. The kinetic energy of the hot steam spins a rotor on a turbine.
5. The rotor spins a shaft.
6. The shaft spins magnets inside a generator.
7. The magnets push electrons in the generator's wire, creating an electric current.

I noticed that changing coal into electricity is a little like changing wind into electricity.

Energy Efficiency

"In every energy transfer," said Rey, "some of the energy changes into another useful form. The rest escapes into the environment. We say it's lost, but it doesn't really vanish. It just isn't used. **Energy efficiency** is how much energy gets used compared to how much energy we put in."

"For example," he said, "when a typical power plant changes coal into electricity, one-third to one-half of the coal's potential energy changes into electricity. The rest of the energy is lost. Can you figure out how?"

Nobody raised a hand.

"OK," said Rey. "Let's observe an energy transfer. Maybe that'll help us."

Rey plugged in some lamps and took off the lampshades. The lamps had old-fashioned round light bulbs. Then Rey handed us each a piece of paper cut into a spiral. He'd tied a string to the center of each spiral. We switched on the lights and dangled our spirals above the lamps.

"What's happening?" he asked.

"My spiral is spinning," I said.

Rey explained, "Your lamp has an incandescent bulb. When you switch it on, electricity heats a thin wire inside the bulb. The wire gives off both light and heat. It heats the air around it. Hot air rises. Air rising from your lamp blows your spiral." He paused. "Now can you tell what happens to most lost energy?"

"It escapes into the air as heat!" I said.

"Bingo," said Rey, smiling. "Remember: even though we talk about 'losing' and 'saving' energy, energy is never lost. It only changes form."

Improving Efficiency

"In the early 1900s," said Rey, "scientists figured out how to make more efficient light bulbs. They're called fluorescent bulbs. They change more of the electricity they get into light and less into heat. Scientists took decades to make fluorescent bulbs small and cheap enough for home use. They finally did it in the 1980s."

Using compact fluorescent bulbs is one easy way to save energy.

Rey took a lamp and replaced its bulb with one that looked like a white coil of glass tubing. "This is called a compact fluorescent light bulb, or CFL," he said. He switched it on and held a paper spiral above it. The spiral barely moved. I could see that the CFL gave off less heat than the other bulbs did.

"A CFL wastes less electricity making heat," Rey said. "So it uses less electricity than an incandescent bulb to make the same amount of light."

"That's cool," I said, "but so what? Is it important to use less electricity?"

"It sure is," said Rey. "Conserving energy helps us keep Earth healthy." ★

WHY CONSERVE?

When people use less electricity, power plants can generate less electricity. Most power plants burn coal or natural gas. Some use cleaner methods, such as capturing the power of wind or water. But no matter what method is used, it affects the health of our planet. Power plants use up Earth's resources or change them permanently. Power plants also add a lot of pollution to Earth's air, water, and land. This pollution harms all living things—including people.

Congratulations! You have learned a lot about energy transfer. You've discovered that energy is everywhere. It's the ability to change matter or do work. You know that energy takes two main forms, but there are also other kinds of energy. Matter in motion has kinetic energy. Potential energy is the energy matter has because of its position or how its parts are arranged. You've learned that energy can't be created, destroyed, or lost. It can only change form or location through energy transfer. You understand that conserving energy is important for the health of Earth and all living things. You can be proud of accomplishing your mission.

CONSIDER THIS

★ Think of some energy transfers that happen in your daily life. What forms of energy are involved? How does the energy change?

★ How do plants change energy from the sun into chemical energy?

* Wind turbines convert wind into electricity. What other kinetic energy in nature can people convert into electricity?
* What happens when two chemicals react with each other? How does your body get energy from chemical reactions?
* This book suggests one way people can conserve energy. What are some other things you can do to save energy?

The Hoover Dam turns the energy of the Colorado River into electricity.

chemical reaction (kem-i-kuhl ree-AK-shuhn) when two substances mix and their molecules break up and rearrange into new kinds of molecules

electron (i-LEK-trahn) a tiny particle that travels around the center of an atom; electrons jumping from atom to atom create an electric current

energy (EN-ur-jee) the ability to change matter or do work

energy efficiency (EN-ur-jee i-FISH-uhn-see) the amount of energy that changes into a useful form during an energy transfer

energy transfer (EN-ur-jee trans-fur) a process by which energy changes form or location

kinetic energy (ki-NET-ik en-ur-jee) the energy of matter in motion

molecule (MAH-luh-kyool) the smallest particle of a material that has the same properties as that material

potential energy (puh-TEN-shuhl en-ur-jee) the energy matter has because of its position or how its parts are arranged

turbine (TUR-buhn) a device that captures kinetic energy to make electricity

BOOKS

Claybourne, Anna. *Forms of Energy*. Chicago: Heinemann-Raintree, 2010.

Landau, Elaine. *The History of Energy*. Minneapolis: Lerner, 2006.

Nemzer, Marilyn, Deborah Page, and Anna Carter. *Energy for Keeps*. Tiburon, CA: Energy Education Group, 2010.

Solway, Andrew. *The Scientists Behind Energy*. Chicago: Heinemann-Raintree, 2011.

WEB SITES

Energy Kids

http://www.eia.doe.gov/kids

Learn what energy is, where it comes from, how we use it, and how we can conserve it.

Energy Quest

http://www.energyquest.ca.gov/index.html

Learn more about energy through videos, science projects, news updates, helpful links, and more.

FILL A BALLOON

Find an empty glass bottle, such as a soda bottle. Put the mouth of a balloon over the top of the bottle. Fill a medium-size pot or bowl with hot water, and set the bottle in the hot water. Watch the balloon expand. What is filling the balloon? Where does the substance filling the balloon come from? Why is it moving into the balloon?

STRETCH YOUR MIND

Hold a wide rubber band with both hands. Pull your hands apart, stretching the rubber band. Aim it away from you and anyone around you. Now let go with one hand. What happens? Why? Fetch your rubber band and hold it with both hands again. Feel the temperature of the rubber band by touching it to your upper lip. Now stretch the band between your hands. Then relax it. Stretch it again and relax it. Repeat this several times in a row. Feel the temperature of the rubber band on your upper lip again. Does it feel colder or warmer? Can you tell why?

INDEX

acid, 15, 17

base, 15

carbon dioxide, 15, 20
chemical energy, 16–17, 19, 20
chemical reactions, 14–16, 20
coal, 19, 22–23, 25
conservation, 22, 25, 26

digestion, 16, 19

elastic energy, 9
electric current, 11–12, 22
electricity, 10, 12–13, 22–25
electromagnetic energy, 20
energy efficiency, 22–24

fuel, 14–15, 19

gravitational energy, 9
gravity, 8–9

heat, 19, 22–25

kinetic energy, 4, 6–8, 12–13, 16–17, 20, 22, 26

light bulbs, 23–25

magnets, 11–12, 22
matter, 4, 8, 26
molecules, 15, 19, 20

photosynthesis, 18–19, 20
plants, 19–21
potential energy, 4, 8–9, 13, 16, 17, 23, 26
power plants, 22–23, 25

wind turbines, 6, 10–13
work, 4, 7–8, 26

ABOUT THE AUTHOR

Christine Zuchora-Walske has spent 20 happy years writing and editing books and articles for children, young adults, teachers, and parents. Her book topics range from animals and planets to history and politics. Christine lives in Minneapolis, Minnesota, with her husband and two children.

ABOUT THE CONSULTANTS

Peter Barnes has always been fascinated by energy and matter in space. For the past 25 years, he has been studying how stars form in the Milky Way, our home galaxy. He lives in Gainesville, Florida, with his wife and two science-loving children.

Gail Saunders-Smith is a former classroom teacher and Reading Recovery teacher leader. Currently she teaches literacy courses at Youngstown State University in Ohio. Gail is the author of many books for children and three professional books for teachers.